VALIANT THOR'
SECRET TECHNIQUE$
CONTACTING SPACE PEOPLE
AND YOUR HIGHER SELF

- by -

MICHAEL X. BARTON

* * *

This is an Educational and Inspirational Course of Study... especially written and intended for NEW AGE Individuals everywhere. The following SEVEN Chapters are contained herein:

1. "THE SAUCER MYSTERY UNVEILED"

2. "BROTHERS OF THE HIGHER ARC"

3. "CONTACTING YOUR SECRET X"

4. "HOW TO UPLIFT OTHERS NOW"

5. "WILL YOU BE A CONTACTEE?"

6. "YOUR MOST IMPORTANT ROLE"

7. "SPACE BROTHERS NEED YOU NOW!"

* * * * * *

Statements in this Course are based on Scientific and Super-Sensory Findings. No claim is made as to what the information cited may do in any given case and the Publishers assume no obligation for opinions expressed or implied herein by the author.

ISBN-13: 978-1518800207
ISBN-10: 1518800203

PRINTING HISTORY
Futura edition published 1959
Saucerian Press edition published 1980
New Saucerian Press edition published 2017

AUTHOR'S FOREWORD

"SECRETS OF HIGHER CONTACT" was written at
the definite request of our Space Brothers.
It is intended especially for you -- the
New Age individual -- to uplift and guide
you on THE PATH OF THE HIGHER CONTACT.

The complete technique by which you may
reach up into the high consciousness of the
Interplanetary Beings and contact them, is
revealed for the first time in this book.
The Brothers --"Beings of the Higher Arc" --
considered it unwise to reveal certain details
of the "Higher Contact" before we were ready.

"SECRETS OF HIGHER CONTACT" contains some of
the best information I have been privileged to
give in my lectures. It also brings you the
latest, up-to-the-minute ideas, conclusions
and instructions for your important NEW AGE
activity in the service of others.

A new phase of the Great Plan is now under
way. Activity on the Flying Saucer horizon
has not ended. It is just beginning! Our
Higher Brothers now wish to make conscious
contact -- via Telethot (special Thought
Transmission) with many thousands more of us
New Age Individuals on Planet Earth.

Your important part in this wonderful New Age
activity is outlined herein. You are about
to open a Door into a fabulous universe.
Proceed carefully and cautiously, following
instructions closely. Do not try to rush
things. Allow yourself time to unfold this
new and wonderful experience.

                              MICHAEL X
                              Seer of The New Age

SECRETS OF HIGHER CONTACT

Part One
The Saucer Mystery Unveiled

A special Message given by Michael X to a wonderful
group of New Age Individuals at Park Manor Hotel in
Los Angeles, California, Oct. 9, 1959

* * *

BLESS YOU, EVERYONE! It's so
inspiring to be here and to see you
again, and to feel the warmth of
this group tonight. It certainly
thrills my soul. And in this feeling, this uplift that I have been
joyously receiving from you, I am
confident that what will come forth
tonight will be something we shall
all remember for a long time.

I pray that the Master that guides me shall be with me
tonight. And I ask that he place his hand upon my shoulder--
give me Light and Strength to share with you. We know -- you
and I -- that he will be here.

Since 1947 when Kenneth Arnold made the first important
sighting of Flying Saucers in the United States, a vast number of sightings and "contacts" have been reported by many
persons. You and I realize that a great many of these reports
have been based -- not on fact -- but on overwrought imagina-
tions and inaccurate observation. People have thought they
were viewing flying Saucers when in reality what they were
viewing was high altitude jet planes, balloons and in some in-
stances the guided missiles of our Armed Forces.

Also, a certain amount of fraud has reared its ugly
head in the Flying Saucer picture. Some of the stories of
contacts with the Space People have been hoaxes. Sometimes
the motive behind the hoax has been mercenary, and sometimes
the motive has been to gain a sense of "self-importance" in
the eyes of the world. All of us know of such cases.

But in spite of fraud, money-grubbi g, and distortion of
the truth, a large number of these reports of sightings and
contacts have been made by reliable, intelligent and honest
people. Capable people whom we love and respect, such as en-
gineers, scientists and important individuals in every walk
of life. These individuals KNOW the TRUTH. They know that
this planet we live on is being visited by interplanetary
craft manned by intelligent beings from other worlds!

And in spite of it all...In spite of so many "imagined" sightings and contacts and fraudulent stories that we have heard to date, all of these things are being used by the ALL Father to further His purpose in these times. The sightings have served the special purpose of AWAKENING the good people on earth to the BIG CHANGES that are coming. Yes, He has been preparing His own, His Elect people for the Dawn of the Day now imminent. The Great Day of this our planet earth.

Now tonight, we are going to talk about the Secrets of Higher Contact. Many of you sincere New Age Individuals have been asking, "How can I contact the Space People?" You want to know HOW to actually become a "Contactee" so that you too will communicate -- as a select few others on our planet are now doing -- with higher intelligences from other worlds.

I assure you IT CAN BE DONE. If your motive is right, you can make higher contact. But, and this is the only real "catch" to it...If your motive is wrong, that is, if it is primarily selfish, you will only make lower contact. That is where so many otherwise sensible persons get sidetracked. They forget to put their little "small-self"will aside, so that the Higher Self in them can act in its pure, noble and unselfish way.

Your High Self is not in the least interested in small or petty aims. It is not interested in personal "self-importance" either. What really matters most to it is whether you are perfectly sincere and honest in your wish to serve the universal forces of Life, Love and Light. Sincerity and honesty enable us to unfold and progress faster on THE PATH.

Many well-meaning persons are "in contact" with lower intelligences and, sad to say, are not even aware of the situation. You may perhaps know of someone who believes he (or she) is in communication with some advanced being from another planet, but the truth might be just the opposite. Some mischievous and wily entity--a lower type of intelligence on the astral plane of our own planet earth--may be posing as a Martian, a Venusian, Jupiterian, Saturnian, etc.

Let me make myself entirely clear on this point. Not all spirits are good spirits. They are not all necessarily good, wise and honest. There is a great astral realm surrounding the earth, and this realm has its lower regions and its higher regions. The lower astral regions are inhabited by beings of less spiritual development than the beings who dwell in the higher levels of the astral realm. Some of these low astral beings like to "masquerade" as wise and superior intelligences and they say to many would-be contactees that they are the higher space people. And many people are being deceived. The deceived ones then go about unknowingly deceiving others.

The reason why these lower intelligences get away with their trickery is easy to understand. They are always on the lookout for foolish men and women with BIG EGOS. Anyone who is puffed up with "small-self" importance is fair prey for those clever astral entities who play on the individual's vanity, pride and basic selfishness. They wedge their way into one's consciousness through the ingress of a bloated ego. Then the lower entities USE that individual to further their own unsavory purposes.

How can you protect yourself against those dark forces? By your MOTIVE. Let it be in line always with the upbuilding forces that exist within all creation. That is easy enough to do, once you become imbued with the spirit of HIGH ADVEN-TURE! Yes, that's the key to it. HIGH rather than low. To seek the HIGH self -- the Oversoul as Emerson described it -- is our objective. Reach for Soul-Contact first. Then, it will be utterly impossible for you to go wrong or contact the wrong type of space intelligences. Your vibration will be too high for them.

That spirit of high adventure in your soul is constantly lifting you upward if you will respond to it. It's always bringing you just the right experiences that will help you develop the beautiful SOUL within you. So reach with me for the "High Consciousness", and with this attitude, with this approach, we shall demonstrate the ideals of High Thought, High Word and High Deed in all that we do.

Then, we find ourselves moving onward, upward and God-ward instead of merely marking time. Our higher vibrations will be just right for making contact with the genuine Space Masters, our spiritually advanced Brothers and Sisters of the more highly evolved worlds. We won't allow ourselves to get sidetracked and delayed on the astral plane. We want to "by-pass" that lower level and reach up to the high contact. From then on, our joy will be boundless.

Service to the Great Plan of the ALL-Father, which the Brothers themselves know and serve, is the crying need of our planet and its people today. The need is -- TO SERVE. And we can all serve the Father's Great Plan best by making a determined effort to reach up for Soul-Contact first. Then, by consciously cooperating with the Hierarchy of Wise Ones in every way that is shown us in our day-to-day lives.

Whatever the Brothers call you to do in these times, by all means put your best foot forward. This is what you and I have waited all our lives for, to lose ourselves -- our little selves, that is -- in a HIGH and NOBLE CAUSE! The time is NOW, and the cause is that of UNIVERSAL UNDERSTANDING!

We have the great opportunity now to cooperate with the Higher Beings in bringing about the Great Plan. That Plan is unfolding according to schedule. We know that the appearance of the flying saucers in our skies in the past few years has been an important part of the Plan. Since 1947 there has been a vast number of true and valid sightings. They have now served their purpose. They have brought about a certain spiritual AWAKENING in the souls of New Age Individuals all over this planet.

Of course, the "mass-minded" have missed the main point of it all. They are still looking for sensation and physical phenomena. But the Brothers are not trying to convince the masses of anything, nor are they concerned with converting any of the skeptics. there isn't time for that. They are, however, greatly interested in reaching the "awakened ones", individuals like yourself because you are teachable.

At the first annual Convention of AFSCA (Amalgamated Flying Saucer Clubs of America) which Gabriel Green held at the Statler-Hilton Hotel here in Los Angeles, the Brothers let us know they and their ships are not "imaginary".

On the very day of the Convention, Flying Saucers were sighted over Hawaii! Perfectly timed for the Convention... remember that? Newspapers carried front page headlines!

So these Higher Beings exist! They are real, advanced human beings, exalted beings with a tremendous intelligence. They know how to time events precisely. And they know how to carry out a great over-all plan for greater human good.

The very fact that you are here tonight; the very fact that I am here tonight is part of a higher plan. A truly spiritual plan that we have the opportunity and privilege to voluntarily cooperate with. No one is imposing their will upon us. Least of all the Higher Brothers. They never impel nor impose their will at any time. Each of us has free choice as individuals. We may choose or reject.

If we can see the Plan more clearly, then of our own free choice we can lay the "small-self" will aside, on the Altar of the ALL-Father. Then the higher will and purpose of the Father begins to work through us. And this is truly the highest wisdom, because the small-self possesses very little wisdom, actually. Far, far grander wisdom exists beyond it!

The Space Brothers say that what we call our "human will" is really only an illusion. The automatic working of the natural law of action and reaction (karma) knocks out the concept of human will. Only the Universal Will exists.

You and I know that every action always brings a reaction, and the reaction is good or not so good depending on the nature of the act. No matter how we try, we cannot avoid the consequences of our actions...but happily we do have a free choice. We can carefully choose our actions.

And when we choose to act according to Higher Self direction, rather than from Lower Self "mis-direction", the higher Will of the Father works through us. With its magnificent power, wisdom, light and love and joy, we are then lifted higher and higher on the TRUE PATH. We UNFOLD THE GOD IN US. It's thrilling, isn't it? And wonderful!

Why then, are the Space Brothers here? Why have the Flying Saucers been seen? The answer now appears that it was to awaken the planet. It was to awaken us (who are now ready to be awakened to our higher destiny) to the fact that we are now in the Last Days of the Old Era. The Piscean Era is fast coming to its closing, and now the New Era -- the Golden Age of Aquarius -- is about to unfold in all of its grandeur and glory.

They -- our Space Brothers -- are here to help us because we are sick. WE ARE SICK WITH KARMA! NEGATIVE KARMA! Karma being the strong reactions from destructive actions we have committed in the past on this planet Earth! There has to be a healing, loving, enlightening force brought in to our world to neutralize the negativity and bring a state of balanced equilibrium NOW.

From that new state of balance, where Light, and Love and Joy predominate, we can function in a healthier condition. We can then become attuned to the Universal Will. In this way we shall find our place in this particular time.

And each of you HAS a particular place -- a unique and special function -- because you are a New Age Individual! You have a high responsibility in these times to serve only your highest ideals. To become a Soul-Center of Light and Love and Joy more radiant and powerful than ever before, so that you can be of greater assistance in the days ahead. I know the Brothers need you and me...and we need them!!

THE TIME OF SIFTING HAS NOW ARRIVED   This is now a great Sifting Time on planet Earth. The Lambs are being steadily sifted from the Goats. Edgar Cayce as he spoke through my beloved friend Betty Nuss, mentioned this -- that the Sifting Time is here now. All of the spiritually awakened souls (the Lambs) on earth are being separated from the goats who are blissfully asleep to the reality of their spiritual nature and the Great Plan.

Those who have become awakened souls -- the Lambs --
will be enabled to assist the Great Army of Light in the
unfolding of the Great Plan for humanity. You and I as New
Age Individuals will become mighty forces for bringing about
that Higher Plan.

A great Cosmic Cycle of time is drawing to a close, and
our planet is getting ready for something higher, better and
far nobler than anything it has ever known. The big changes
coming will mean a step upward for this earth and its people.
It will all be brought about in as gentle and natural a way
as possible...for that is the way the Higher Forces work.

These are conclusive days that we live in now. When
the realization of this fact reaches your inner self, are
you fearful? Don't be. You must let go of fear and replace
it with joyous love and gratitude for all that is in the Plan.
Conclusive days, yes. But not the days to walk with fear.
For you and I have a greater opportunity in these times than
we have ever had in all of our previous lives on earth! An
opportunity to walk in the light, love and joyous awareness
that we are -- all of us -- "watched by angels", and that
they are working with us and for us as we REACH UPWARD.

THIS IS THE   "Many shall be purified," made white and
TESTING TIME   tried at this time, as never before.   Tried to
               see IF they can be relied upon as responsible
co-workers in the "vineyard of the ALL-Father". Now to be
a reliable co-worker means simply this: That we voluntarily
offer to lay our personal "small-self" will upon the Altar
of the Sacred Spirit -- the Divine Spark within us. We set
the little human self aside, and ask the Higher Self to take
control. That is what it means.

Giving up the little self-will is not easy to do. Few
of us can release it all at once. Each day we have to give up
a little more of "human mask" of personal "self-importance"
and desires of the personality, for something BIGGER, BETTER,
AND ETERNAL. We are not ready for HIGHER FREEDOM until we
place our Divine Spirit in control for only it is FREE.

In our new freedom we go into ACTION...here and now.
We apply what is given to us, each step of the way. Deeds,
not words are most important to your progress and mine. We
go into action at once to purify ourselves, to cleanse our
etheric bodies, to lighten and transmute our bodies of flesh.
Remember, we are gradually entering into a New Dimension on
this planet Earth. It will become a planet of higher vibratory frequency, of more etherialized matter. We cannot rush
things. But we can and should move with the Cosmic Tides...
and with courage prepare now to move into new dimensions.

oooOOOooo

- 8 -

SECRETS OF HIGHER CONTACT
Part Two

Brothers of The Higher Arc

Soul-Contact is the MOST IMPORTANT thing we could possibly do at this time for ourselves and for others. This is so vitally important now. Why? Because the High Self intelligence of each individual is his or her best teacher and guide.

Your soul is able to communicate with the High Self, and carry on a two-way conversation with it. Thus will you receive the most valuable higher wisdom and guidance. For it is the still, small voice speaking within you that can lead, guide and direct you clearly in the way you should go as you travel THE PATH.

With such divine guidance -- for it is actually the voice of God speaking to you -- darkness and confusion is dispelled and you move swiftly on the true path of LIGHT.

At this time -- as the Old Piscean Age is rapidly drawing to a dramatic ending -- walking with those in the Light is important. Walking in the Path of Light is very important. And walking in the Path of Love...that is MOST important! Love is the Key to reaching up into the High Consciousness. Yes, it is a fact. Higher Contact is made only by those who love, for love lifts us into a very high awareness.

Many New Age Individuals are sending a great vibration of pure love out to other human beings at this time. This is most helpful, for as we realize, the "Sifting" of human souls is now going on. During this Sifting Period we try to help the "goats" to come up into a higher state of awareness.

Only a very few of them will understand and respond. As for the others of the "mass-minded" men and women, they will not understand what is going on right under their very eyes. But you -- and all other New Age Souls -- you shall understand. You shall keep faith with your teachers and with your higher self. The human goats will continue moving in circles because they are depending on physical, material senses only. They must see, hear, touch, smell and taste in order to believe.

Unhappily, such persons are "trapped" in matter. They lack inner vision to see the spiritual realities that exist behind material things. When "D-Day" - Diploma Day -- comes, those spiritual laggards will not be entitled to a "Diploma" attesting to sincere, higher service to mankind; because no such service has been rendered by them. But do not feel undue concern over those souls. No soul is ever lost in the Great Plan. Laggard souls are simply "harvested" by the Etheric Beings in charge of such things, and taken to a planet in another solar system where conditions are more in keeping with their "slowpoke" nature. On that less evolved planet the backward souls will "take the work over".

You, the New Age Individual, by your study and practice of these higher teachings, are spiraling up beyond the "trap" of dense matter and its limitations. You are moving upward into a faster vibration to where the Light from your High Self can pour through you in ever-increasing radiance!

Soul-Contact then, is the next step to take. And the magic of higher contact is simply this: That first of all, before seeking to contact the Saucer Beings, we are to make genuine contact with our own Soul. Via the Soul, we reach upward to make contact with the High Self intelligence.

Then, having done that -- and we do it by daily practice of certain techniques of Light now being revealed to all the faithful -- the other contacts with Saucer Beings will follow in a natural, easy sequence of steps.

Each of you has a most wonderful opportunity now to become a more perfect and useful "channel" for the Light, and a marvelous "receiver" of higher communications. According to your sincerity of motive and desire to be of service to the "Brothers of the Higher Arc" will you become a center -- a living center of Life, Love and Wisdom.

In this regard I must speak of the Subliminal State of mind. It has an important relationship to higher contact. The Subliminal state is a condition of "conscious plus Subconscious awareness". When you acquire the art of relaxing your physical body completely, you find that your mind gains greater freedom. Although your conscious mind is still to some degree active, your deeper mind, the subconscious, is most active. Gradually it begins to function throughout the entire brain. You are no longer hampered by little hindering ideas, and soon you experience a HEIGHTENED AWARENESS.

Edgar Cayce, the Seer of Virginia Beach, became quite proficient at entering into the "Subliminal State" of mind. That state led him gently into the higher, or "Superconscious State" of mind. "Super" meaning above and beyond, or a higher state of awareness. Wisdom then poured through him and he was enabled to assist many thousands of sincere individuals, by giving them psychic readings as to the real nature of their physical ills, and the best means of treatment.

In my earlier book entitled "Venusian Secret Science", the complete technique of getting into the subliminal state was presented in easy-to-understand step by step procedure. Those who haven't yet learned this important technique which is very basic to any contact with the higher forces, should secure this valuable information as soon as possible.

Now, we come to a very interesting subject: Definitions. How do we define "Space People"? For some time now, many of us have used the term "Space People" or "Space Beings" in referring to all beings who travel in the Flying Saucers and in the various types of spacecraft. This is true; these are "Space people" defined as those who are able to travel safely in outer space. The fact is, however, that there are many different kinds of beings who inhabit space. Human beings, for example, who have attained mastership over matter by working knowingly with Light (and that includes mastery of their finer bodies) are able to lay aside the heavy material body and travel in a mental body. They can then move with the speed of thought. All space is their home and they do not require physical or etheric spacecraft in order to navigate anywhere in our solar system. Can we not call these "Space People" also?

There are also Etheric Beings. These are human dwellers on the various etheric planes in the universe. They live in worlds just as real to them as ours is to us, but they have no dense material flesh body as we do. These, too, are space people.

There are also the WATCHERS. In the Holy Bible they are called "Watchers from a far country". They are physical human beings very similar to us, whose home is not on earth but on some other material planet in our solar system. In order to reach our planet they use spacecraft of an advanced type which are capable of interplanetary flights. Although they have physical bodies, they are of a much higher vibratory frequency than most earth bodies and are far more "etherialized".

Most of these Watchers come from the more highly evolved planets such as Venus, Mercury and others. They have been observing our planet since 1947 in a most intent manner. As you have already learned, they are aware of the critical condition our planet is in now that it has the secret of atomic power. Atomic radiation due to the many atom bomb tests has caused more havoc than most of us realize. But that is not all.

We now live in a COSMIC TIME. Our entire solar system is entering a new and higher region of light. Changes of a cosmic nature are definitely due for this planet and for us.

In the days of Noah people were told to "flee to the high mountains". Now we are not told to flee to the mountains but rather to "stand in the Holy Place". Where is the Holy Place? It is within you. It is the Sacred Shrine that each individual now must build within himself. For within that Shrine shall come the "telepathic call", the warning, the guiding and the leading from your own High Self Intelligence.

Divine direction will come. Your responsibility and mine, is to diligently train ourselves to be better "receiving sets" for higher thoughts and impressions. In ancient times the word given Ezekiel was: "Behold, Son of Man, I set thee a Watchman to warn my people!" Yes, the Watchman will warn us at the proper time. But it will be an inner warning, an inner voice rather than an outer voice. And it will come through the mechanism of your own awakened Soul.

We said that these are conclusive days. Magnificently big changes are impending. The Brothers of the "Higher Arc" are far more aware of the nature of these changes than we are. That is why many high and noble beings from extremely high and spiritual realms are coming to our planet, and why they have been observing our world for so long. They desire to be near this earth, to better assist us in these conclusive days. And here is a most important point.

These High Brothers I now refer to are Etheric Beings. But they come from an Etheric level infinitely higher and more refined in Etheric Density than any of those surrounding this planet earth. Their order of intelligence is far greater, and far more spiritual than anything known to us.

These wonderful Beings have made the great sacrifice of taking on themselves an Etheric body much denser, and much heavier than the fine spiritual bodies they normally wear. They themselves do not call this a sacrifice...but they say that perhaps you or I would term it that. They use denser bodies to be near us at this time. It is not easy nor comfortable for them to be in earth's lower vibrations, but as it is necessary for us to be guided, they have come.

They are near us, guiding us, leading us. Why? To enable all sincere souls to perfect themselves and enlighten others. As we do this, we shall realize what St.Paul was speaking of when he said: "And we which are alive (in our higher frequency perfected bodies) will be caught up into the air to meet Him." This event is the "Great Airlift" spoken of in the Bible and in other sacred books.

If each one here tonight will put forth the sustained effort that is required to REACH THE HIGH CONSCIOUSNESS, I assure you that you SHALL make the grade! Your spiritual light will begin to shine with ever-increasing brightness. THAT bright light will positively attract the attention of the "Brothers of the Higher Arc". They'll see your light and draw closer to you. Then high contact will become a reality to you. A glorious, living reality. YOU WILL THEN BE A "CONTACTEE". And all your doubts will be gone.

The Brothers, of course, become interested in you only when they observe that your light is shining brightly. For they know that you are then READY to contact them, and that your motive is pure and that you are reaching upward to them for GREATER LIGHT. Believe me, they are happy to receive you!

Remember, however, that it is far more important for each of us to find the "voice of God" within us, and be guided by that voice than to depend upon any other person or persons. In our upward journey into LIGHT, LOVE and LIBERATION, we are assigned higher Teachers to assist us. Their duty is to aid us in making our own inner connection with the "Diamond Star" --the Soul-Center within our own hearts.

So never lose sight of that purpose. You will enjoy the loving companionship of many wise and noble Teachers as you travel the UPWARD PATH. They will imbue you with a zeal, fervor and enthusiasm you've never before experienced! You will thrill with joy and gratitude, for their light will enable you to carry out your particular job at this time and in the days to come. I tell you it will be THRILLING!

LIGHT IS NOW INCREASING FOR OUR SUN SYSTEM IS ENTERING NEW REGIONS OF LIGHT   People everywhere on the planet are starting to wake up to a new STIMULUS... Some understand it. Others are still in the "dark" as to its source and meaning. The amazing fact is, our entire solar system with all of its planets, is moving into new and powerful regions of light in God's universe. It is the sign that we are nearing the close of the Old Dispensation and stepping boldly into the NEW ERA. As we do so, the intensity of cosmic light energy is being increased to such a degree that those who are on the side of LIGHT will express constantly greater light and "inner knowing".

In fact, sincere New Age souls will SHINE with light, so that their very bodies and garments will radiate MORE LIGHT. But those who are on the side of the "goats" will become ever darker and darker in their desires and ideals. I believe I can give you an example of this condition right now. Try to find a bright, cheery, light-colored suit of clothes in a department store nowadays. It's almost impossible. Everything is such a dark, sombre color. The "Continental Look"

is the latest fashion now, for men and women. They're bringing it over here from Europe. For many people it will be just
the thing. For me...no thanks! I still prefer the lighter
colors. They symbolize the Light. They uplift. This is, we
all know, the time of cosmic light. The time when great light
should illumine and beam from all of us! Especially in America.

The karmic history of Europe is by no means good. The
continent is in certain portions quite decidedly "Old Age".
Our friend Edgar Cayce gave one of his remarkable psychic readings in 1934 in which he said: "The upper portion of Europe
will be CHANGED in the twinkling of an eye.."

As the great light gradually increases there is greater
contrast between those "in the light" and those enmeshed in
materiality. So do not be alarmed if you are misunderstood by
the multitudes (and your relatives). They have not awakened.

We are aware -- you and I -- that NOW is the time for a
great INWARD PREPARING. That is why we have been gathered
together with one united purpose. To CONTACT THE LIGHT. To
get ourselves attuned -- our mental television sets activated
-- so that we are enabled to know and commune with the Guiding
Minds of the spiritually advanced Teachers.

We live in a great time. There is a great and glorious
destiny just ahead for all true New Age individuals. We are
going to realize that glorious destiny...mark my words. All
of us Sons and Daughters of Light, in one strong and united
body, are moving onward, upward and Godward. And as we move
upward under the higher direction of the Brothers and our own
High Self intelligence (which gives us an open line direct to
our Creator God) we become MIGHTY TORCHES OF ASSISTANCE!

Your flame of LIGHT will become so bright that it will
enlighten and assist a countless number of "New Age souls" who
are only waiting for your light to uplift them. But it is also
your divine responsibility, as a New-Age Individual, to <u>maintain</u>
<u>inner poise</u> <u>and</u> <u>control</u> in all of the higher activities you en-
gage in. Poise, control and balance must be your guideposts
now more than ever. <u>Find</u> <u>your</u> <u>own</u> <u>center</u> <u>of</u> <u>Christ</u>-<u>Balance</u>
<u>within</u> <u>yourself</u> <u>first</u>. Then reach upward to commune with the
higher beings. Express always in love from your Soul-Center.
That will keep you balanced and harmonious at all times.

Guard against emotional imbalance, for over-excitability
hinders clear thinking. Develop a deep inner calm and peace,
for that is your assurance of protection from the Wise Ones.
Walk this Path, reach UPWARD in thought and love, and you too
will know the MAGIC of higher contact. Then, with this Wisdom,
all the Powers of Light will walk with you!!

oooOOOooo

SECRETS OF HIGHER CONTACT

Part Three

Contacting Your Secret X

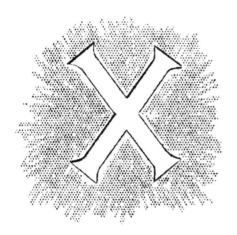

The first step to take on the wonderful path that leads to "Higher Contact" with our Space Brothers is this: making "X" contact. It is so important to all who are desirous of consciously communicating with those inhabitants of other worlds, that I cannot over-emphasize it.

What is "X"? Simply a symbol for your own highest spirit-self. It is the high-self intelligence of you.

X, as we all know, is used in mathematics to stand for the "unknown factor". The unknown factor in my own life for many long and bewildering years was my Higher Self. I was like countless other persons on our planet, totally unaware of the existence of my high self. It is exceedingly difficult -- if not impossible -- to become aware of one's higher self when one's ordinary human self demands all the attention.

In 1940 I had a most unusual and startling experience which brought me "face to face" with my unknown higher self. I had never, previous to this time, had any kind of contact with a living Master or Teacher from another planet. I was, however, a deep and serious student of the "hidden secrets" of life. My bookshelf bulged with "occult" books of every description--- and yet -- I had never touched reality.

One night after reading a chapter or two of an advanced and complicated treatise dealing with "White Magic", I turned out the light in my bedroom and went to sleep. It was my usual bed-time -- ten o'clock -- and sleep came quickly.

I slept for several hours. Then, at about 2:00 A.M., I suddenly was aroused to full conscious awareness. Something strange and unusual was about to happen. I sensed that what was about to occur would be of deep soul significance. In a few moments my premonition was confirmed.

As I lay there on my bed in the darkness of my little room, opening both eyes to see whatever I could in the dark, it happened. A tall, graceful being in the form of a man wearing a light flowing robe, quietly entered through the closed door and walked over to my bedside. Yes, he had walked right through the

solid door and as he stood beside me, I felt my own body begin
to tremble. My eyes seemed riveted upon the remarkable being
who had just "stepped into" my life in this unusual manner.

He was indeed extraordinary. Tall, well proportioned and
majestic in his appearance, I had only to look into those amazing eyes of his to know. Here was a being of marvelous power
and intelligence. His entire body radiated a beautiful light
so that I could see him easily in the dark. It seemed to me
that little rays of light shone from his large eyes which
sparkled like blue diamonds. The calm expression on his face
indicated perfect balance of strength and love and high intelligence. And yet -- I was excited and afraid.

Why? I do not know. Perhaps fear comes too naturally,
too easily to the majority of us earthlings. Maybe that is why
we get into fights and yes, wars so frequently. For me, in
those early days, fear was an emotion I had not yet cast out
of my consciousness. I felt that emotion then.

The tall Master -- for such he most certainly was -- had
no intention of disturbing me further. At once he became aware
of my fear and with a gentle, understanding smile upon his lips,
turned around and was soon gone.

Then came the voice of my own Higher Self -- soft but clear
-- "Be not fearful of your Teachers. Learn the lesson of higher
love. See harmony within all creation and build a greater realization of oneness with all living beings. In this perfect
love all fear is dissolved."

That was a big lesson for me to learn. And it was not
until I had really transmuted fear into the higher love that
the "Brothers of the Higher Arc" could reach me and teach me
other important lessons. Keep this in mind as you continue your
progress as a New Age Individual seeking higher contact. Love
is the realization of oneness. It is the soul's sincere desire
for health, harmony and happiness within all beings.

Don't, for heaven's sake, be like me -- so upset that I
actually "frightened" my teacher away! When your time for
meeting a marvelous being from Venus, arrives, by all means
try to maintain your composure. There is no good reason to be
afraid of any advanced human being who sends out the wonderful
vibration of higher love to you. On the other hand, if the
"harmony vibration" is missing in your contact with any being
of advanced intelligence, be careful. It is possible for us
earthlings to contact advanced beings who are advanced mentally
but not spiritually. My advice is to always be wary of any intelligence who is "all mind, but no heart". There are such, contacting earthlings, but these are not to your highest welfare.

It is your privilege and responsibility to "test the teachers" before following their suggestions or advice. How do you test them? Very simply. By the trinity principles of Power, Love and Wisdom. Our Brothers of the Higher Arc -- especially those from Venus -- always bring about a beautiful and "balanced" effect when they communicate with you. That is because they never over-emphasize one aspect of the trinity at the expense of the other two. When they apply Power they use an equal amount of Love and Wisdom at the same time.

This causes their thoughts, feelings and actions to be harmonious, positive and joyously constructive. No matter what Teacher you contact, either on the mental, the astral, or the physical plane, test him or her for BALANCE. If you sense inwardly that he is bringing inharmony into your soul by an imbalanced vibration, he is NOT your true Teacher.

Regarding all contacts with the Brothers, a word or two of caution. Never be frivolous. Frivolity is out of place, because it indicates disrespect. Communication with higher beings from advanced worlds is serious and of the deepest importance to you and humanity. Reaching the mind of a Space Brother from Venus, for example, is no simple matter. There has to be a very close "attunement" of both soul and mind before the condition of rapport is achieved between you.

Here is the basic procedure to follow:

1. Whole-hearted desire. You must desire to contact the Brothers of the Higher Arc, with a deep-souled intensity.

2. Belief in them. You must feel in your heart that the Brothers exist just as you do; that they can respond to you.

3. Be Sincere with yourself. Ask yourself, "Why do I desire to contact the Space People?" Purity of motive and Sincerity are the attitudes which will protect you from unwanted, lower entities and vibrations. They are your "shield and buckler".

4. Raise your vibrations. Body, Soul, Spirit have to be raised to a new and higher level of awareness. Your awareness must rise above earth's sphere until it reaches the High Arc of Venus or other advanced realm of human life.

I have learned that the Venusians, and all of the many other higher beings, are in close touch with their own "X" or Higher Self. They are "in tune" with its BALANCED-LIGHT principle. This is the balancing and illuminating factor from which comes all wisdom. And that is why Earthlings who desire to know and serve the Brothers, should practice identifying themselves with their High Self ("X") first. By doing this and by not

identifying yourself with your desires, or your emotions, a
great change will take place in you. No longer will you feel
yourself to be an insecure, limited human personality. You
have changed your identity. Of your own free choice you have
accepted the "X" (higher self) as your true self.

However, this is only the beginning. Your individual soul
will not be able to hear the soft, still voice of your higher
self until you have first slain the Dragon of Desire. This
does not mean that you should "kill out all desires". Not at
all. It does mean that you must not permit yourself to be so
tossed upon the stormy sea of emotions, passions, appetites and
personal desires that the beautiful voice of your higher self
cannot reach your ears.

To contact your Secret "X", it is essential to bring more
tranquillity, more balance and more self-control into all thoughts
feelings and actions. Here is how to do this. As you go about
your daily activities, no matter where you may be or what you
might be doing, think of your Secret X. Think of it as a perfect
blend of Light, Love and Life. Or if you prefer, as Intelligence,
Harmony and Power. A balanced trinity. Think of it with joy.

When your trinity of Power, Harmony and Intelligence are
blended in your consciousness so that they become one unit, that
is when you may reach your Higher Self. Then it is that you may
hear the voice of your own immortal spirit whispering within your
soul. Practice listening at least once daily for that voice of
your own "X". Early morning is the very best time to contact it.
The moment you waken from your night's sleep, listen quietly in
silence and calmness for some message from your higher self.
Learn to commune with that high source.

The Space People -- Brothers of the Higher Arc -- have long
since learned to live and think and express from their Secret
"X". To them there is nothing mysterious, nothing difficult
about this. They recognize it to be simply a "unified consciousness" composed of the three higher principles. Namely, Intelligence, Harmony and Power in balance. They say there is indeed
a "Shining Presence" within each one of us, regardless of whether
we happen to be Earthlings, Venusians, Mercurians, Martians,
Jupiterians, Saturnians, or so forth, ad infinitum.

The "Shining Presence", they say, is the glorious result of
our consciously blending the triad of Intelligence, Harmony and
Power into a more complete and perfect Self. Because the inhabitants of Venus and other advanced worlds have discovered the
magic of their own Secret "X" and attune all of their thoughts,
feelings and actions to its harmony vibration, you will find
that the most effective way for you to communicate with them will
be to attune first to your Secret"X". Thus affinity will exist.

ooo000ooo

SECRETS OF HIGHER CONTACT

Part Four

How To Uplift Others Now

The Venusians say that Higher Love is the keynote of the coming New Age. Why? Because Higher Love seeks Balance and Balance is the great secret of Harmony, Peace, Health and all Wisdom. This higher love is different from earthly love.

Earthly love is important. But it is so often binding us instead of releasing us into greater freedom. The reason it does so is because it generally lacks the "balance" factor, and is based more upon self-getting than self-giving.

Higher love frees, releases, harmonizes everything it contacts. It is not "possessive" nor restrictive. Rather it brings you a realization of "oneness" and a joyous, harmonious freedom that makes your heart sing in gratitude. When you come into this happy feeling it is like warm sunshine beaming down upon you from above. You feel its gentle rays and want to bask in that sunshine of Higher Love forever.

When man on our planet comes into an understanding of this higher love -- to the point where he desires harmony, health and happiness within all creation -- then he will be ready to reach out to Venus and other worlds and extend the hand of love to them. The Lord Thinkers of Venus will then welcome and embrace us openly. But you know as well as I do that the highly spiritualized minds on advanced planets are not going to stand for any childish attempts by earthment to "conquer" outer space through brute force. No indeed.

The Lords and Teachers of Venus are very wise. War and violence have long since been banished from their glorious world. It is the planet of the Christ-Love principle, and they intend to keep it that way. Gently but firmly they tell us that a realization of higher love is essential before the "astronauts" of earth will really master interplanetary flight. Until we are willing to extend a hand of love to them, we shall continue to "miss our target" time after time.

The first requisite is to practice giving freely of our higher love vibration. When you desire within your heart and mind and soul to harmonize, unify and uplift any person or situation, you are sending out the right vibration. It is a desire or yearning for a condition of exquisite harmony, wellbeing, and happiness to exist within all living beings. That is higher love. Give freely of it. Expand your love to take in all races all men, women and children on all planets as one great brotherhood. Then we shall all be working together in harmony for the unlimited GOOD of all humanity. As you and I and all New Age souls express more love -- not the self-getting variety, but the freeing love -- all men and nature will work together joyously in Cooperative Brotherhood. This is the way of love. It is the way to uplift others now.

Are you often greatly puzzled as to how you may best assist your friends and loved ones who do not realize these "New Age Truths" the way you do? Here is the answer. You CAN uplift them into a new, higher and happier vibration by doing THREE things for them:

> 1. Bless them by recognizing silently that each soul is a center of Light, Love and Life. Mentally project to them an image of themselves as being lifted into a new vibration wherein they see the "Shining Presence" of their own beautiful Higher Self.

> 2. Send the clear thought of Peace and Good-Will to those persons you wish to assist. Mentally "spray" their auras with uplifting, pacifying thoughts of peace on earth, Good-Will to all living beings.

> 3. Send living energies of color by visualizing these from yourself to those you would help. Colors of the light pink, green, blue, violet, etc. are powerful soul-energizers. Each color has a specific energizing or releasing effect.

These three simple things to do for others will make a definite, constructive change in anybody and everybody involved in this noble activity. Not only do the sender and receiver benefit, but the good vibrations go out to uplift, harmonize and add joy to the entire planet. This will assist all other New Age individuals to make higher contact with their "X" and with the loving souls of Venus. And it will assist you to make contact also, for harmony and balance are the keys to all higher communications. The more who do these, the greater the uplift.

We do not have to use our mental or will-force to tell a person to "do this" or "do that", but just simply send out to him or her the positive vibrations of Peace and Love. And bless that person so he will become aware of his True Self and awaken into a new and wonderful consciousness.

The Space People have clever ways of illustrating their ideas. Once they showed me a picture of a large block of ice in which a fish had been frozen. Nearby was a large axe. Now,

how could I release that fish from his prison of ice? My first
thought was to grab the axe and chop into the block of ice.
"That would be like imposing your will," said my Venusian Mentor. "But what would happen? The axe might cut into the ice
so deeply and sharply that the fish would be injured or killed."

Then the answer to the problem was presented. All
that I needed to do was to place the block of frozen ice out in
the direct sunlight. The sun's warm rays melted the ice and
freed the captive fish. No force or violence was required.

To release any person from some negative condition, all
you need to do is remember that little lesson of how the fish
was freed from its state of suspension. Souls too, get sus-
pended in low vibrations, in discord and illness. They are in
a sense frozen in ice, like the fish. While in that negative
condition of suspension they cannot make progress. But you and
I can help by sending them love. Love melts the ice.

When the ice melts, the soul unfolds and awakens of its
own accord. On this planet we are to help one another unfold,
and the finest way to do that is by sending out the vibration
of love in the color essence of rosy, radiant pink. Tincture
the color well with golden light. A dark shade of color is not
too helpful. It doesn't give the uplift, and the souls all need
this uplift into the higher vibration. Pink color has this up-
lifting effect. Also, it assists in bringing about a state of
well-being and optimism to others. It lifts them up. They begin to see life through "rose-colored glasses" as it were, and
this is wonderful, for it sets them free of discordant thoughts.

In sending out this cosmic love vibration, visualize a pure
white light pouring down into you from above. See it entering
through the top of your head and filling your heart with a gold-
en white radiance. Now visualize that golden white radiance in
your heart turning into a golden pink. As soon as you become
aware of the pink color, send it out with full power to the one
or ones you wish to help. Send it out from your heart center
to theirs. See the pink color going out from you and wrapping
itself as a radiant mantle around the heart center of another
and awakening that heart into a joyous new freedom. This will
release them into harmony that will permeate their words and acts.

By sending the high love vibration of this golden pink light
to your friends and loved ones, you will be doing them a tremendous service which will help to wipe away a great deal of Karma
that you may have accrued through your own past incarnations on
this planet Earth. And though you may not at once notice the
difference in the appearance or actions of the one you have thus
helped, have patience! We have seen this technique succeed time
and time again.

oooOOOooo

SECRETS OF HIGHER CONTACT

Part Five

Will You Be a Contactee?

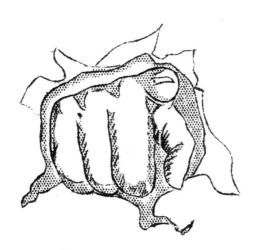

THE ANSWER to that important question is YES. I am quite certain that you -- if you yourself choose to be a Contactee, will become one. How soon depends upon your sincerity of motive and your faithfulness...

Our Space Brothers tell me they desire to make conscious contact with more and more individuals in all walks of life. The reason they desire this is because they have a Great Plan that they are serving... a wonderful Plan, powerful and cosmic and universal in scope.

That Plan is simple in essence, but complex and intricate in its ramifications. The average earthman's mind is not "geared up" to grasp this Cosmic Plan, because as yet we have not advanced to this higher octave of being that our Space Brothers and Sisters have realized. It is so wonderful that they have an earnest desire to contact more and more of the New Age souls that are now awakened.

Now, at the present time on this planet, there are already more than 100,000 awakened souls. The goal, say the Space People, is a minimum of from six to ten million who are fully aware of their presence and purpose here. Since 1944 (three years prior to Kenneth Arnold's sighting) the Brothers of the Higher Arc came in a great host into our atmosphere, to fulfil what they call a fifty year plan in the higher interests of Earth and its people.

With great caution and wisdom, these Brothers did not reveal to any one individual the entire workings of the Plan. One by one they have been contacting the "awakened ones" of earth, and teaching them a certain part of this wonderful Plan of theirs. Bit by bit the pieces have been gathered together, until now at last it is shaping up and we can see the great overall picture much more clearly for the first time. Not even the Contactees knew the vast scope of this Great Plan, but now the complete picture is being released. The Plan is so big it requires a great dedication of each New Age soul to tell others, so that we can uplift more of humanity...into a new octave of vibration. That is the goal. You will find a few clues in your seventh chapter of the Book of Revelation. And if you think there are only 144,000 "saved" souls, read the second half of that chapter!

The Creator has a mighty Plan. The Higher Brothers are consciously cooperating with that Plan, just as you and I may do when we become more aware of it. The Plan includes not only our planet Earth, but all of the Planets in our Solar System. It is a Lift, an uplift in the vibratory frequency of this entire Solar System. It is a Cosmic Upgrading of the Planets and their inhabitants. And although the big change may come suddenly, Nature is leading up to it very gradually, just as she does in all her work. There is a period of growth and preparation and finally the "fruition". We are now approaching that time of fruition.

That is why souls on earth are awakening now. Never before in history have more people begun to LOOK UP to the wise beings from other worlds for guidance and instruction. We realize -- you, I and many others -- that something BIG is impending... something of COSMIC MAGNITUDE. Something that touches each and every one of us deeply, whether the laggard souls accept it or not.

That's why you yearn for Higher Contact. You are seeking actual connection and attunement with the Creator's Plan. You wish to align yourself with that Great Plan and with the Higher Brothers because they are themselves aligned with it.

The way is simple, easy and without force. It is simply a beautiful blending of the principles of Intelligence, Love and Power in a beautiful harmony. This is the real key to Higher Contact, because you see, Higher Contact is just that. You are stepping up into a wonderful NEW vibration -- a higher Dimensional state. A Dimension that will thrill you to the very depths of your soul when you attune harmoniously.

This thing is Master-Minded. Each awakened soul -- and we said that there are about 100,000 now -- has a special role to play in this mighty New Age drama. It is principally the job of awakening and harmonizing other souls. But no two of us will serve in the same capacity. Each will have his or her own unique manner of serving the Big Plan, so there will be practically no duplication of roles.

As more of us find our place in this activity -- and no New Age individual is happy until he does -- we will start to raise the "mass consciousness" in a wonderful way. The awareness of the masses of people on this planet will be stepped up, and this, our Brothers say, is the way it will be.

We will not ALL be awakened, but millions of us will be. Millions of us will be "Contactees". You very likely shall be one of these, secure, loving and enlightened by the Brothers. You'll be centered and poised in the mightiest principle of ALL. The mighty principle of the BALANCED LIGHT. That is the beautiful balance of Love, Power and Wisdom within YOU.

Are you ready for Higher Contact? Yes, if you yourself
are certain that your reason, your motive for contacting the
Space Brothers is pure. Purity of motive is most important
and this means simply that you are not seeking to contact the
Brothers merely to satisfy a curiosity. Curiosity-seekers are
really selfish souls who are more interested in their own little personal desires than in serving the Great Plan. Any self
seeking motive keeps one's soul-vibration in too low an octave
of vibration. That hinders all higher communications.

Therefore, clarify your real motive first of all. With
purity of motive (serving the highest Universal Will and Purpose) you then should devote 5 minutes in the morning, 5 minutes at noon, and 5 minutes at night to conscious recognition
of your own "X" or Higher Self. The Higher Self dwells on a
plane above your Human Personality and is always attuned to the
CHRIST-BALANCE LIGHT in the universe. And here is the SECRET.
The more of that BALANCE-LIGHT you receive from your Higher
Self, the more perfectly balanced you will be in body, mind and
soul. With balance you are much better able to carry on a most
intelligent and perfectly rational conversation with the Space
People, who are highly advanced mentally and spiritually.

VERY IMPORTANT: Call for the BALANCE-LIGHT every time you
think of your secret "X". Ask that the light be sent down from
the high self into your brain and into your heart center. This
marvelous practice clears your mental "channels" for communications via Telethot (telepathy) from the Brothers.

The Space Brothers do want each and every one of you to
BE a Contactee. They are confident that you CAN become one.
This is in the Great Plan you know. It is high time, they say,
that earthman awakens from his dream and connects to REALITY.
The Balance-Light is tremendously real. Our Space Brothers and
Sisters are real. So are their Celestial Ships in our skies.

A Contactee must anchor himself to realities at all costs.
To follow the siren call of fantasy, imagination and make-believe
will only result in self-delusion and imbalance. Before we reach
for contact, we seek first the Balance Light. And the more that
Light of your "X" is invoked and welcomed into your body as outlined in this book, the more perfectly balanced you become. Then
as you reach up to make the thought communications with the High
Beings, you work in harmony and poise. There is no imbalance
of mind. It becomes, in fact, better balanced.

Becoming a Contactee is your New Age privilege. Now is the
time to apply these secrets given you for your higher progress.
If you will invoke the Light as directed, if you will use great
zeal in carrying out instructions, you WILL BE A CONTACTEE.

oooOOOooo

SECRETS OF HIGHER CONTACT

Part Six

Your Most Important Role

You have played many important roles in your past lives upon planet earth, but your biggest role is just ahead. In simple words, it is this: You -- as an awakened New Age soul -- are needed to assist in the liberation of this planet.

More than 100,000 men, women and children in all walks of life, of all age groups, are now beginning to "liberate" those around them...and the ranks of our mighty Army of Love, Life, and Light is growing by leaps and bounds!

You belong to this New Age Army of Light. You, dear friend, are one of the Liberators of mankind. What are your important duties? To Balance, Harmonize and Interpret the present and coming events in the light of your New Age knowledge!

Of course there are many key figures in this movement. In the foreground among the Flying Saucer enthusiasts are the Con- tactees -- those men and women who have made mental or astral or physical contact with Spacemasters from far distant planets. Most of these Contactees have written books telling about their amazing experiences. They also lecture before the various Flying Saucer Clubs and New Age organizations.

I have -- as one among many Contactees -- received vital thought communications from the Space People. I have told of my various contacts from the public lecture platform in many cities here in California. Book after book has come forth from my typewriter, in accord with the wishes of the Space Brothers. But I say to you now...heart to heart and soul to soul...it is not the writing of books nor the lecturing that is most impor- tant in the liberating, the freeing of humanity.

In your New Age service, you may write or lecture. But those are to be secondary activities. Getting in touch with the Space Brothers comes first, and this means you must qualify for communication. Prepare yourself to be a crystal-clear channel for their messages and directives. Then, when they contact your mind and soul, there will not be interference from your Lesser Self which would confuse their message.

Not everybody can qualify as an author or public speaker, and the Brothers say that is not the main issue anyway. The big thing to do right now, individually, is to consciously and voluntarily ALIGN OURSELVES with the Great Purpose of our Creator. "Tuning-in" on that purpose is our prime objective.

Now, I have good news for you. Due to the upliftment of the thoughts, feelings and actions of all of you during the past few months, much negativity that would otherwise have manifested on this planet has been to a great extent nullified. We are making headway. The positive Balance Principle of Inner Harmony is being anchored in every city, large and small, of EVERY STATE in the U.S.A. Inner harmony creates Outer harmony.

We desire harmony. Why? Because we know great changes are imminent. We must have the Balance-Principle well anchored in our minds and hearts in order to hold the balance in the days ahead. Our individual efforts to do this are most effective.

We know that a great cold spell just recently went through our country in the midwest and Great Lake areas. Chicago staggered under a siege of cold that hit 30° below. People died there through the intense cold. Climate everywhere has been changing considerably in the past few years...more than we've ever noticed in previous times. One man said to me when the weather in California was very hot, unseasonably, that it seemed like Heaven "with Hell just around the corner!" Something sinister impending.

The truth is, it is not at all sinister, but COSMIC. And none of us need have any fear whatsoever of these changes. "When ye see these things come to pass, lift up your head and rejoice, for your redemption draweth nigh." This is what Jesus told His elect. Who are the elect? Those who elect (choose) to AWAKEN. Our Brothers keep telling us over and over again that Higher Love -- the Christ-Balance Principle -- casts out all fear. It harmonizes the environmental conditions and keeps you protected.

That's why many awakened souls are sending out this Love Blessing -- not the sickly, sentimental love that is generated by weaklings -- but a powerful, balancing and unifying energy that, if need be, could SAVE A CITY. Multiply that immortal "New Age Energy" by several million and it can actually SAVE A WORLD... This is your NEW AGE ACTIVITY.

These are your instructions: Anchor the Light, the Balance Principle in your heart and mind firmly. Hold the personality or human self OPEN always to any inflow of power, light or wisdom from your Higher Self. Free your physical body and your etheric body of any impurity, shadow, cloud or obstruction to the Light. Each of us must cleanse our bodily vehicles of impurities so that the Light can flow freely into us without resistance and without causing pain. Let New Joy replace old shadows!

Act One of the great world drama began with the awakening of humanity to the fact that interplanetary beings exist. Act Two -- world liberation -- now begins and YOU are needed!

oooOOOooo

SECRETS OF HIGHER CONTACT

Part Seven

Space Brothers Need YOU Now!

Yes, a totally new and marvelous phase of the Great Plan --which the Brothers themselves know and serve -- is now beginning to unfold. It is WORLD LIBERATION. It is the second act in the mighty drama that involves every one of us.

You are needed to assist the Space People in liberating mankind from its hopeless burden of negative "Karma". Here is what they desire you do do now!

(1) Condition yourself now for conscious contact, mind-to-mind, with the Venusians and other Brothers of the Higher Arc. Do this by purifying your MOTIVE first of all. In purity of motive is the GREAT SECRET of making Higher Contact. And the purest motive is simply this: To follow in perfect accord with the Plan of that Great Being we call our Creator. He has it all figured out. And that Plan is coming down from high spiritual sources through the great Balance-Light. It is the purest white Light known and we call it the Christ-Balance Light.

As your innermost motive then attunes with the motive of the Creator, your light expands. And as it expands, the Brothers will become aware of it and will then come to you to assist you. At first they will guide you gently, without your knowing it, perhaps. Later, as you grow stronger and more valuable to the cause you will be contacted telepathically and receive instruction and "working orders" direct from the Brothers themselves.

(2) Of your own free choice -- never because of what I or anyone else says -- begin to adopt a more vital, natural, and meatless diet. How and what you eat will affect your ability to "tune-in" with the Space Brothers. You can raise or lower your personal vibrations by the kinds of food you put into your stomach. Here is what happens: The eating of meat or flesh foods causes a dark shadow or cloud to form upon the etheric body. The etheric body is the pattern or sustaining vehicle upon which the physical body is built. A person with clairvoyant vision can at onc once perceive the dark cloud that forms on the inner body when one eats meat. This cloud acts as an interference or obstruction to the Balance-Light that is sent down from the High Self. Unless the Light from your High Self can get through easily, your vibra-

tion remains too low in intensity for clear and easy communication with the minds of the Space People.

As you gradually make the required change in your diet, re-
placing fish, fowl and flesh with protein from non-toxic sources
such as almonds, sunflower seeds and other vitalized foods..and
open yourself to the inflow of Light...the cloud that may now
be obstructing your Higher Contact will start to dissolve. Now
I myself found that until I did change my diet, thereby raising
my vibrations, I was unable to make Higher Contact even though
I had a great desire to do so.

But to make any changes in diet -- or even in your own
thinking -- without having the urge to do so coming from within
your own self, of your own free choice, is apt to produce conflict. And you can never go two ways at the same time success-
fully. It tears you apart. I realize that many would-be Contactees as well as you who may already be Contactees, have a certain
amount of conflict within yourselves. The Brothers are asking
you to go in one direction and your personal will is tugging at
you to go in the opposite direction.

This situation must be resolved without conflict.
When we begin to embrace the Great Purpose of the Guiding Mind
that brought us into being -- and that directs the Cosmos --
then the conflict of the small-self-will dissolves.

You will find this: That if you will make the effort to
set aside the small-self-will and reach up for this greater Light,
Love and Power coming now from the Creator, an amazing thing will
happen. The Space Brothers, who give the details of this Great
Plan to New Age individuals, will help you to "connect up" with
the Light of your High Self. It will then become easier and
easier for you to set aside your little will for something far,
far grander and nobler. You will find one day, that the smaller
will has "melted" or submerged itself INTO the Greater Will!

Then, as more Light pours into your brain and higher centers
(pituitary and pineal glands) you will notice a wonderful new
mental clarity. The thoughts of the highly intelligent beings
of Venus and other advanced worlds will then come into your consciousness clearly.

(3) When your light shines brighter you will be seen by the
"Brothers of the Higher Arc". One of them -- your present Teacher
on your individual ray -- will get in touch with you telepathically. This will happen only at the proper time. When it occurs,
do not be startled nor alarmed. It is most important for you to
observe the following practice. Obtain for yourself at least one
(two would be better) psychic gems or stones. You will use them
to assist you in raising your vibrations sufficiently high to

enable you to project your thoughts, and commune with our marvelous Space Brothers.

The Gem Exchange, Bayfield, Colorado will send you a complete list of recommended psychic stones for this purpose. A postcard to Mr. S. N. Green, Owner of the Gem Exchange at Bayfield, Colorado will bring you a quick reply and details about the "Telolith" Stone which I fully endorse.

It is essential that all psychic gems, crystals, etc. be first "purified" of any mixed magnetisms of low vibration and then spiritually "charged" with a high potency Light from the High Self. The crystal or psychic stone then becomes imbued with the Balance-Light vibration of the spiritual self. This is a powerful aid to contacting our Space Brothers, since the "charged" stone steps up your capacity to receive as well as transmit thoughts. All that is necessary is to place the charged stone upon the head so that it is directly over the pituitary gland. Unless a psychic stone is properly de-magnetized and charged with the Light power from the High Self, it is not fully effective for Higher Contact. (See Venusian Secret Science, end pages.)

(4) Set aside a regular time for Higher Communication. It is preferable to have this "Contact Time" just after you rise in the morning, and before breakfast. It should always be at the same time each day and in the same room. Now, at the exact time you have chosen, sit down at your desk or table with pen and pad ready. Hold your pen so that only penpoint is lightly touching the paper -- no part of hand or arm should touch. Your objective is to contact your Cosmic Teacher mentally during the next 15 minutes. When contact is made, he will use your arm to write his name first. (Let the pen move freely of its own accord. You may sense a kind of electric impulse prompting movement in your arm.) If the name is slow in coming, mentally request your Cosmic teacher to give you the name he wishes to be known by. He will do so if you have qualified for communication with him, by the new brightness of your own light. And he may also identify himself to you by means of a special symbol uniquely his own. As an actual example, my present Mentor uses the name Ramel and identifies himself by the sign of the Golden Ram. With the sign comes an individual vibration which no other being can duplicate, for no two beings have the same vibration, as all of them (and us) are individuals with different soul and spirit patterns.

Your teacher will identify himself clearly and positively at the first successful "Contact Time". At the end of your contact, say that you are ready to discontinue if agreeable with the Teacher. Wait until he signs off by giving his name, before you leave. This "sign-off" procedure is important and must not be neglected. It insures against the entrance of possible lower entities at this point. We are not endorsing "automatic writing" as such, and later on, your teacher may not need to

write thru your hand, but will communicate entirely by telethot.
You will know when to discontinue the "writing" because you will
begin to get more and more of your teacher's inspirational words
or ideas, or even "picture-thoughts" which you will be able to
recognize as coming from your teacher. So the writing may stop.

But you will use your regular time for Higher Communication.
And you may continue using the Telolith and other psychic "aids".
When using the Telolith, do not try to hold the stone in place
with your hand. Either "tape" it to your forehead between the
eyes or place it on top of the head, using a lightweight cap
over the stone to keep it in place while you are concentrating
on the communication. Next, mentally surround yourself with a
golden white light. Visualize it pouring down from above into
your entire body and immersing you in a great Tube of Light.
This is your protection against undesired low vibrations.

Your Venusian Insignia (for details see list at back of this
book) should be in sight in the room where you communicate daily.
Now, put your full attention upon the Venusian Insignia for a
full five minutes. As you gaze quietly at the tiny spot of pure
white at the center of the Insignia, centering your attention
upon the white spot, soon the muscles of your eyes will relax
slightly. You are inducing a condition known as the Subliminal
state of awareness. In this condition you will become more sen-
sitive to the thought energies of the Space Brothers. So the
Venusian Insignia is a true contacting device, having the advan-
tage of being a definite physical object. Therefore it is a
better "attuning link" than a mental image, for most persons.
All physical aids can be dispensed with later, but not until your
"attunement" has been well established.

After gazing quietly at the Insignia for five minutes, close
your eyes and slowly count to seven. With each count, mentally
request your consciousness to rise higher and higher. Without
this "stepping stone" stepping-up process, mental contact is much
more difficult to achieve. After mental contact has been achieved
and the teacher has "signed off" by giving his name, begin count-
ing IN REVERSE from seven back down to ONE, slowly. Then with
open eyes, stamp your foot once on the floor to assert symbolical-
ly that you have returned to normal state of consciousness. Under
no circumstances should you neglect this!

These are the secret techniques you have been waiting for.
Put them to work for you at once. Do not feel discouraged if you
fail to make contact immediately. It merely means that you must
continue invoking the Light and raising your body vibrations, in
your daily life. Like any other reward in life, Higher Contact
must be earned. THOUGHT, FEELING and ACTION always working together harmoniously and in balance at the highest level will prepare you for this great experience. I urge you to reach up! Now!
For the Higher Brothers are calling you.

ooo000ooo

"THE COSMIC QUESTION BOX"

By MICHAEL X   EXTRA SPECIAL BONUS

Q.1.   How soon will I be contacted by the Saucer People?

A.   This depends upon you. Our Space Brothers are making
        mental contacts now with those individuals who are in
advance of the majority of the people. You can earn your contact by following directions carefully. In time ALL New Age
individuals will be contacted.

Q-2.   Is two-way telepathic communication with the intelligent
        beings of other planets possible?

A.   Not only is it possible, "Contactees" in all parts of the
        world are doing it. At present time, most of this Tele-
thot communication is done at a relatively short distance between
the spacecraft in our atmosphere and us on earth.

Q-3.   What are the benefits of contact with Space People?

A.   Tremendous new mind and soul freedom through contact
        with powerful and advanced intelligences..beings who
have actually connected up with the big universal realities!

Q-4.   Can every sincere individual become a Contactee?

A.   Sincerity is very important. However, purity of one's
        motive is the biggest determining factor. Our Space
Brothers know they can accomplish their good purpose only by
carefully choosing those who are mature enough in soul to be
loyal and dedicated cooperators in the Great Plan.

Q-5.   Will my Space Teacher communicate with me in English?

A.   He will communicate in whatever language is most famil-
        iar to you.

Q-6.   Are there many different types of Space People?

A.   (1) Physical beings whose vibratory frequency is consid-
        erably higher than ours, (2) Etheric beings who dwell in
        the etheric regions around the earth and around other
planets, (3) Celestial beings involved in the cause side of creation (Angelic Beings.) The first two classifications are made
up of our Elder Brothers and Sisters who have already advanced
to the next "Hier Arc" of Soul, mind and Body progress. They
make use of Spaceships, Space Stations and mental contact methods.

Q.7.   Does life on Venus resemble our life on Earth?
A.   Yes, but more spiritual, more perfect, more glorious.

- A -

Q-8. How may I be sure it is really my Space Teacher who is
     in contact with me telepathically, and not my own mind
speaking to me?

A.   First, you will notice a rapid delivery of ideas to you
       when a Brother of the Higher Arc is in contact with you.
Your own mind is not generally as definite and swift in its
functioning. Second, the knowledge your Space Teacher gives
you will be completely unlike anything you are now aware of

Q-9. How can I protect myself against lower intelligences, for
     example, beings from the lower astral planes?

A.   Like attracts like in the mental realms. If you keep
       your physical, mental and soul vibrations high through
high thought, high feeling and high deed...your aura and mental wavelength instantly repels and wards them off. It is up
to you whom you will commune with, just as it is up to you to
make the decision as to which associates you prefer. Purity
of motive protects you best, because it permits more powerful
Light from the High Self to flow into your body. Low entities
cannot tolerate the higher vibration of that Light.

Q-10. Why are the Space Brothers contacting us?

A.   For World Liberation. They are cleaning the astral realms
       inside and outside of our earth, and freeing our minds
of "Old Age" concepts. This new and higher phase of their work
-- contacting as many of us as possible -- is in line with their
purpose of preparing this planet and our people for the coming
"Initiation in Light".

Q-11. Why is it that the good has such little effect on the
       bad in our world? Why is there so much wrong on earth?

A.   Because earthman -- generally speaking -- has not yet
       accepted voluntarily the Christ-Balance way of life.
Man does not consciously recognize the importance of keeping
harmony within all nature. His own soul is asleep to the universal realities of limitless LIFE, LOVE and LIGHT all around as
well as within himself and in all of creation.

       Simply put, Man has ignored the God-Plan of Higher Love.
In its place earthman has substituted his own egotism and personal will to dominate and conquer all creation -- including
outer space -- by mental cunning and sheer physical might. He
has thereby greatly imbalanced his thoughts, feelings, and actions. Most men -- our leaders in high places included -- see
only the outer, material appearances of things. It is the small
minority of wise humanity who are now aware of inner realities
or "soul" purpose within all things. We must hold the balance.

Q-12. Is Venus really inhabitated by human beings?

A.   YES. This is so. Venus is inhabitated by the more ad-
        vanced occult souls. It is the home of human glorified
beings of happy, joyous students leading an exalted human life.
The Teacher we know as Jesus lived on Venus before his birth on
our planet Earth. They have physical bodies, but of a much
higher vibratory frequency than ours, and they radiate more
Light at all times. For further information I refer you to my
book: Venusian Secret Science, and to the testimony of such re-
spected teachers as Helena Blavatsky, Max Heindel, Alice Bailey,
and Rudolph Steiner.

Q-13. Who will go to Venus?

A.   Venus is the planet of Divine Love, the Christ-like Love.
        Only a mere handful of earth's humanity have awakened to
this high vibration of perfect love. Only the more spiritual
and selfless souls of earth are ready for Venusian life. However, all those who are now actively developing an awareness of
the Higher Love, the Harmony vibration, the beauty and oneness
of all life...are preparing themselves for Venus.

Q-14. Do certain stones or psychic gems make contact easier?

A.   Yes. Edgar Cayce recommended the Lapis Lingua stone, and
        I endorse the use of either that or the "Telolith" crystal
or both. For free ctatlog on psychic gems for this purpose,
write to: THE GEM EXCHANGE, Bayfield, Colorado.

Q-15. I do not feel that I am able to "charge" my Telolith
        psychic stone with sufficient spiritual energy to make
it most effective for contacting the Brothers. Can you help?

A.   Properly "charging" any psychic stone requires that the
        person charging the stone be able to invoke a spiritual
Light Power from his high self and infuse it into the stone.
This does require a definite ritual, as well as ability to in-
voke the high spiritual energy for purposes of good.

        To have your Telolith, Lapis Lingua, or other psychic
gem fully charged by me, here are your instructions: (1) Lay the
stone on a sheet of paper, and with pen or pencil, trace a clear
outline of the stone on the paper. It is not necessary to send
the psychic stone to me. SEND ONLY THE OUTLINE OF THE STONE,
TRACED ON PAPER. I DO NOT REQUIRE THE ACTUAL STONE! (2) Print
your name and address in handwriting at top right corner of the
sheet. (3) Write a letter "X" inside the outline of the stone.
(4) Mail the sheet of paper together with a Love Offering of
one dollar to - Rev. Michael X, Box 38594, Los Angeles 38, Calif.

oooOOOooo

- C -

Afterword

In the "It Can Now Be Told" Department, we may now reveal that the spaceman who contacted Michael X. Barton was none other than the enlightened Venusian thinker, Valiant Thor. Unfortunately, this sleight-of-hand was necessary at the time, due to heightened Cold War tensions and various threats that had been made against Thor and his family, who were working hard to end nuclear bomb testing on Earth. Since Barton was a popular New Age personality in the Los Angeles area, it was crucial that he be among the first Earthlings contacted.

Barton's contacts came prior to Valiant Thor's forced internment in the Pentagon between 1957 and 1960, after which the Thor family became more circumspect about working with citizens of our planet. As such, this book is a bit of a time capsule, highlighting the warm, helpful feelings that Venusians once had for Earthlings. Thor, in particular, is known for having worked closely with Nikola Tesla, sharing all the knowledge he could with that advanced human, even though some of it may have skirted the fringes of galaxial law (which states that we should merely observe underdeveloped species, rather than actively intervene on their behalf).

As we reprint many of the books that we first published many years ago, it should become obvious that Valiant Thor was never totally imprisoned in the Pentagon. As mentioned in Dr. Frank E. Stranges' "Stranger at the Pentagon," Thor could sneak out anytime he wanted. And he did so many times, in order to spread, to various contactees, the anti-nuclear message that was so important then - as it is now.

Luckily, Thor succeeded, and was able to convince world leaders to pull back from the abyss of all-out nuclear war. Unfortunately, his good friends John F. Kennedy, Martin Luther King, and Robert F. Kennedy were all assassinated, setting us back greatly in our efforts to become an enlightened society. We are still struggling with the forces of ignorance and intolerance today.

The work of Valiant Thor and his Venusian associates was obviously of great importance in helping mankind through a difficult time. What we will ultimately do with the many concepts that Thor gifted Tesla, Barton, and others is, of course, still up in the air. But, so far, so good. I ask my readers now to continue supporting the

endeavors of these courageous Venusians. May we all someday experience a world free of fear and war, and enjoy our birthright as free
citizens of this galaxy.

-Gray Barker, 1980

Epilogue

I first encountered Michael X. Barton in the early 1950s, in the Los Angeles area. Dr. Frank E. Stranges had called me on a secure line aboard my ship, Victor One, asking me to "check a guy out" on behalf of the U.S. government. He mentioned that this was security protocol "XX," which meant we were to take certain measures to protect our identities.

During my meetings with Barton, I used a Venusian nickname I had acquired during my childhood, "Lon-Zara." Almost no one on Venus knows me by that name, and the number of people who speak Venusian on Earth is extremely low, so the idea worked. Barton never suspected that I was Valiant Thor.

This was good, because it allowed me to dissipate the tensions between Barton and Dr. Stranges. Barton, it seems, had come to the attention of the FBI because he had been disseminating materials regarding Nazi flying saucers, and the FBI was pressing Stranges for information. Barton was writing about actual technologies being secretly used by the government - areas falling under the National Security Act of 1947.

Some of these developments were certainly nuclear, and involved the companies that built the original atomic bomb. These companies, Barton claimed, had colluded with the Nazis in developing the bomb and building the first flying saucers. They had actually stolen many of Tesla's patents, right after he died, and transferred them to the company now officially credited with building the bomb.

The mention of Tesla's name had a huge impact on me, for I had worked together with Tesla many times, going back even to his childhood. In fact, it can now be revealed that I was actually one of Tesla's mentors and teachers. He was undoubtedly we Venusians' most favorite human being. He embodied the potentials that Earthlings have, but often do not use - potentials that you share with us as genetic relatives.

I asked Barton what he was working on next, and he said he wanted to do more "New Age" books, about health and wellness. I suggested we do a book on Venusian health and science secrets, and the result was outstanding. I reported back that Barton had merely stumbled onto some "Nazi UFO" drawings that a friend of his, in the aerospace industry, had discovered at work. Barton was not at fault, and he seemed to be a "patriot."

Because of this, I worked on more books with Barton (such as this one, "Secrets of Higher Contact") and developed a close friendship with him. I actually believe that our friendship may have been one reason I was detained at the Pentagon. My (unpopular) stance was that the material Barton had found was true (I knew it to be true myself), and so, therefore, it was the fault of the government for not "keeping its nose clean" or protecting its nuclear secrets.

I began to realize that not everyone in the government is acting for the full benefit of mankind, and that it is up to us to forge stronger intergalactic bonds. I therefore confessed to Michael Barton that I was Valiant Thor, and asked him for forgiveness for the deception. He understood, and it drew us even closer. Today, he lives happily with the Venusians in an undisclosed location. He has been experimenting with our secret methods, such as life-extension, and it seems to be working so far.

-Valiant Thor, 1980

Made in the USA
Middletown, DE
26 November 2018